NEW PRODUCT INTRODUCTION

A Systems, Technology, and Process Approach

J. David Viale

A FIFTY-MINUTE™ SERIES BOOK

CRISP PUBLICATIONS, INC.
Menlo Park, California

NEW PRODUCT INTRODUCTION
A Systems, Technology, and Process Approach

by
J. David Viale
The Center for Manufacturing Education

CREDITS
Managing Editor: **Kathleen Barcos**
Editor: **Michael Koch**
Production: **Barbara Atmore**
Typesetting: **ExecuStaff**
Cover Design: **Daniel Barny**

Copyright © 1998 by Crisp Publications, Inc.

Printed in the United States of America by Bawden Printing Company.

http://www.crisp-pub.com

Distribution to the U.S. Trade:

National Book Network, Inc.
4720 Boston Way
Lanham, MD 20706
1-800-462-6420

Library of Congress Catalog Card Number 98-70115
Viale, J. David
New Product Introduction
ISBN 1-56052-492-8

This book is printed
on recyclable paper
with soy ink.

10 9 8 7 6 5 4 3 2 1

LEARNING OBJECTIVES FOR:

NEW PRODUCT INTRODUCTION

The objectives for *New Product Introduction* are listed below. They have been developed to guide you, the reader, to the core issues covered in this book.

Objectives

❏ **1) To discuss improvements in new product introduction.**

❏ **2) To explain necessary key business documents.**

❏ **3) To discuss changing organizational structures.**

❏ **4) To present the major phases of new product introduction.**

Assessing Your Progress

In addition to the Learning Objectives, Crisp, Inc. has developed an **assessment** that covers the fundamental information presented in this book. A twenty-five item, multiple choice/true-false questionnaire allows the reader to evaluate his or her comprehension of the subject matter. An answer sheet with a summary matching the questions to the listed objectives is also available. To learn how to obtain a copy of this assessment please call: **1-800-442-7477** and ask to speak with a Customer Service Representative.

TO THE READER

This book is a resource for anyone involved in the New Product Introduction (NPI) process. Its objective is to help teams, departments, and businesses of all sizes to standardize and improve their new product development efforts in order to bring new products to market faster, at lower costs, and with more value added.

No matter how process-oriented your organization is, there is always room for improvement. By using the information and tools presented in this book, you will:

- Have a list of the key phases involved in the NPI process

- Develop your first pass of your own NPI project plan

- Have a list of over 90 tasks to be included in your NPI project plan

- Develop performance measurements to keep the NPI process on track

- Have a list of the roles and responsibilities for each NPI team member

More specifically, you will develop an understanding of:

- The competitive issues that force companies to formalize their NPI process

- The key business documents and organizational structures that support the NPI process

- The key financial measures that determine the cost-effectiveness of the NPI process

- The vital role of continuous process improvement in the NPI process

- The importance of good project management and team-based organization

Wouldn't you like to beat the competition to market without increasing your cost? Wouldn't you like to attract and keep new customers and increase your market share through better quality at lower cost? Wouldn't you like to reduce lead time and cost of materials through better management of the NPI process? This book will provide you with the means to do that, and more.

ABOUT THE AUTHOR

J. David Viale is the founder and president of the Center for Manufacturing Education, an international training, education, and consulting company. His background includes working for Arthur Andersen and holding management positions at Hewlett-Packard and Fairchild Semiconductor. He used to be a practicing CPA and is certified in production and inventory management (CPIM).

Mr. Viale is the author of the APICs best-selling books, *The Basics of Manufacturing* and *The Basics of Inventory Management.* His most recent book is *JIT Forecasting and Master Scheduling, Not an Oxymoron.* To order these books, go to www.cfme.com or send an email to CFME@aol.com.

If you have comments, ideas, or recommendations, you can contact Mr. Viale at:

(408) 973-0309 (voice)

(408) 973-1592 (fax)

www.cfme.com (web)

CONTENTS

MODULE

I

Forcing Improvements in New Product Introduction

WHAT IS A NEW PRODUCT INTRODUCTION PROCESS?

A new product introduction (NPI) process consists of a series of standardized, overlapping development phases that enable companies to develop and introduce new products in a timely and cost-effective fashion. Each phase consists of a well-defined beginning and ending point and measurable criteria for successful completion. This detailed breakdown enables the NPI team leader or project manager to monitor progress against pre-established goals, identify the scope and nature of potential problems in the NPI process, and assign responsibility for resolution to NPI team members.

THE BENEFITS OF A NEW PRODUCT INTRODUCTION PROCESS

Most companies, especially if they are young, are product focused, concentrating their R&D efforts and resources on their slim product lines. Over time, if they are successful, product lines expand, and often multiple R&D centers evolve. Naturally, each center develops its own way of managing the new product development effort. This lack of standardization, combined with increases in product complexity and variability, results in tremendous inefficiencies that threaten the competitiveness of the business. As markets grow, more competitors enter the scene, and eventually cost reductions and even faster time-to-market pressures become critical for the survival of the company. The result may be an increase in revenue, but a decrease in profit (and quality) because of inefficient new product development efforts.

One way to counteract this situation is to develop a common NPI process. A standardized NPI process helps people better understand their roles and responsibilities. It reduces organizational conflicts and costs and enables teams and departments to be more efficient and productive. This results in a reduction of the time it takes to bring new products to market, which, in turn, results in an increase in profit margins and market shares for the company.

In short, there are tremendous benefits that can be gained from implementing a rigorous NPI process, including:

- Increase in productivity

- Reduction in costs

- Reduction in product development times

- Increase in product quality

- Increase in profit over the product life cycle

- Increase in customer satisfaction

To better gauge these benefits, it is important to understand the major challenges facing businesses today.

TODAY'S TOP EIGHT BUSINESS CHALLENGES

Companies today are under tremendous global pressure to reduce their product development times and costs without sacrificing quality. If you want to stay competitive and make a profit, you must:

1. **Bring products to market faster**

2. **Reduce your costs**

3. **Deliver high-quality products**

4. **Be flexible and open to change**

5. **Develop an informational organization**

6. **Improve your employee training and education**

7. **Improve your information exchange systems and networks**

8. **Improve your forecasting accuracy**

Let us look more closely at these competitive issues that are forcing companies to formalize their NPI processes, and discuss what you have to do to stay in business.

TODAY'S TOP EIGHT BUSINESS CHALLENGES (continued)

1. Bring Products to Market Faster

Products are coming to market faster and faster. As a result, the life cycle of products decreases, leaving less and less time to recoup the investment and earn a profit. For companies to be successful, products must be profitable sooner to secure funding for the next generation of products. To remain competitive, you must gauge your success based on these new measures:

► **TIME TO MARKET:** How fast can you get the product to market?

► **TIME TO VOLUME:** How fast can you produce at a volume that attracts enough revenue to cover costs?

► **TIME TO CONSUMPTION:** How fast does the customer make the decision to buy?

► **TIME TO PROFIT:** How fast can you generate revenue that exceeds cost?

► **TIME TO CHANGE:** How fast can you make changes to accommodate customer requests, and how much do these changes cut into your profit?

2. Reduce Your Costs

To maximize profits, you have to reduce both tangible and intangible costs. This can be done by:

► *Reducing the costs included in the NPI process.* For example, reducing the number of engineering change orders (ECOs) frees up funds that might be better spent elsewhere (tangible costs).

► *Reducing the amount of time included in the NPI process.* Try reducing the number of decisions involved in the new product introduction, as well as the number of authorizations needed to proceed with the project once a decision has been made (intangible costs).

► *Reducing the defects and variability in the NPI process.* (Could be both tangible and intangible costs.)

► *Reducing wasted time.* Frequently time is wasted when NPI team members are not used to their full capacity, because they have to do tasks that others should be doing. Time is also wasted by sitting in unproductive meetings, playing telephone tag, redoing work, frequent interruptions, and so on (intangible costs).

Note: Intangible costs are the biggest obstacle to getting the product to the customer faster.

3. Deliver High-Quality Products

Quality and the ability to measure it play a crucial role in improving a company's capability to go to market faster. For companies that have been able to maintain a "quality mindset" in their products and processes while responding to the tremendous time pressures of bringing products to market, success has been forthcoming. For those companies that have opted for the "ship-and-get-market-share-and-fix-defects-later" approach, the results have been dismal. The key is to improve quality on an ongoing basis through the philosophy of continuous process improvement (CPI). CPI refers to an ongoing process that strives to identify a problem, determines its root cause, and then takes corrective action so that it doesn't happen again. When everyone is involved and processes continually improve, quality improves, costs go down, profits go up, and new products reach the market faster.

4. Be Flexible and Open to Change

You will never be able to control change, but you can manage it. Change is manageable if your organization can anticipate it and respond to it. Change is manageable if you build awareness among your customers, suppliers, and teams of the costly nature of change, and then work with them to minimize it. Change is manageable if you are able to input and analyze it, and then, based on what it does to development cost and schedules, make decisions as to what course of action to follow. Good communication and excellent project management skills are prerequisite to managing changes in the NPI process. Remember, companies that are best at managing change have a competitive advantage. (For more details on change and how it relates to the NPI process see Module V.)

TODAY'S TOP EIGHT BUSINESS CHALLENGES (continued)

5. Develop Informational Organizations

The organizational structures within companies will have to change in order to support an increasing number of products with increasingly shorter product life cycles. Profit margins, returns on investments (ROIs) and returns on assets (ROAs) will have to be reached within increasingly shorter periods of time. To cope with these pressures, there will be at least two organizational structures in every company: (1) the traditional *formal* organization, characterized by multiple layers of authority (including president, executive, and management); and (2) the emerging *informational* organization, characterized by a less hierarchical, team-based decision-making environment that integrates suppliers as well as customers into an interconnected series of organizational structures, all dedicated to supporting the NPI process and bringing products to market faster. Many companies have realized that the more people are involved in the decision-making process, the more likely the product will be delayed. Within the informational organization, fewer levels of authorization are involved in the decision-making process. As a result, products come to market sooner. (For more details on formal and informational organizations see Module III.)

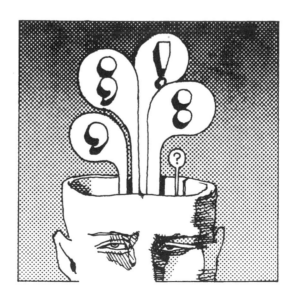

6. Improve Employee Training and Education

People and their ability to make decisions will become a bottleneck if they lack proper training. To increase your company's ability to bring products to market faster, everyone in your company needs to be trained and educated in all facets of the NPI process, including business and financial issues, continuous process improvement, and team building and teamwork. Customers will expand their purchases based not only on your products and processes, but also on your employees' education and training at all levels, including the executive levels. All too often, executives spend significant amounts of money on educating and training their employees, while neglecting their own need for remaining current. As a result, many find themselves making decisions about issues of which they have little or no understanding. The solution? Participate in the training. This is a wonderful way for them to reinforce and train as they learn from their employees. Ideally, everyone in your organization should educate everyone else. Ask yourself, "What person in the organization or department would I least like our customers to talk to in terms of understanding our NPI process?" This is the person to be educated and trained first. Education and training may be the ultimate competitive weapon a company has. (For more details on these issues see Module III.)

7. Improve Information Exchange Systems and Networks

Information exchange systems also create a bottleneck. Change is happening so fast that information systems can't keep up. More advanced information exchange systems and networks must be developed to enhance the flow of information. In order to make better decisions, you need to get information faster. The company manufacturing systems, such as Manufacturing Resource Planning (MRPII) or the expanded version called Enterprise Resource Planning (ERP), must be integrated with the engineering design software package, as well as interface with the suppliers' and customers' MRPII systems. The result will be an enormous increase in the amount of information being generated internally as well as externally by customers and suppliers alike. Needless to say, this accelerated flow of information also results in a demand to make good decisions even faster. It is possible to have a situation in the foreseeable future where data is being generated so fast, it can no longer be converted into information fast enough for individuals to make well-informed decisions about new products. With the Internet, we may already be there. All the more reason to make sure that everyone in your company is properly trained to deal with these new realities.

TODAY'S TOP EIGHT BUSINESS CHALLENGES (continued)

8. Improve Forecasting Accuracy

The major causes of poor customer service in terms of on-time delivery are inaccurate customer forecasts, a multitude of changes to the original customer orders, and an overall lack of account management—not suppliers, not purchasing. The result is excessive inventory, which can ultimately lead to inventory write-offs, high product costs, and lower profit margins. Part of the improvement process is to build awareness with customers of the costly nature of change and what it does to profit margins and schedules. Forecasting must start with the NPI process. The time to improve the accuracy of the marketing forecast is before the product is introduced. The more accurate the individual product sales forecasting is, the smaller the forecast error, and the less inventory needs to be carried to maintain a specified level of customer service. By carrying less inventory, the capacity of machines required to build products is better utilized. Inventory is not built before it is needed, thus avoiding the mistake of committing capacity of machines too early. By carrying less inventory, less space is used.

EXERCISES

In the following exercises, you are presented with three statements and three charts that support the potentially contradictory views, NPI "costs" versus NPI "schedules." Look at the trade-off between project cost versus project schedule and make appropriate recommendations.

EXERCISE 1:
Project Cost versus Project Schedule (Part I)

Review both statements, then write down the ramifications of each statement followed by your recommendations.

1. Products that go to market late, but on budget, earn one-third less profit over five years, while products that go to market on time, but are 50 percent over budget, earn only 4 percent less profit.

   _____

   _____

   _____

   _____

   _____

   _____

2. The later in the NPI process an ECO is written, the greater its impact on the NPI schedule.

   _____

   _____

   _____

   _____

   _____

   _____

EXERCISES (continued)

EXERCISE 2:
Project Cost versus Project Schedule (Part II)

Review Figures 1-1, 1-2, and 1-3, then indicate the ramifications of each chart on the NPI process followed by your recommendations.

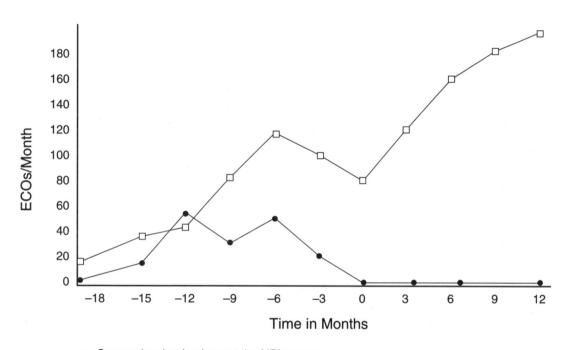

● Companies that implement the NPI process

□ Traditional environment

FIGURE 1-1. *Engineering changes before and after development.*

_____

_____

_____

_____

_____

_____

Figure 1-2 presents a traditional R&D environment, showing that at the completion of the design phase, while only about 25 percent of the development program cost is expended, 80 percent of the product cost is "locked in."

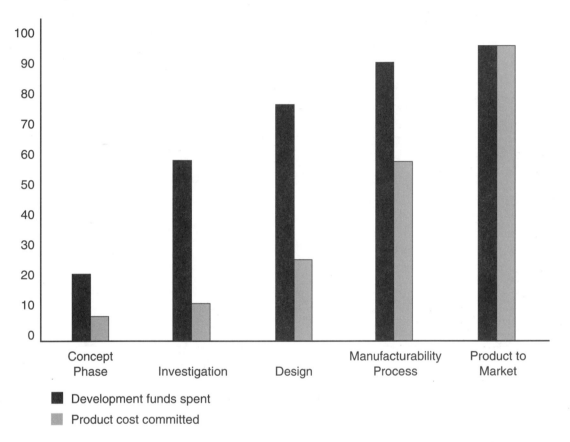

- ■ Development funds spent
- ▨ Product cost committed

FIGURE 1-2. *Amount of project costs committed compared to the degree to which the design is "locked in" during the NPI process.*

EXERCISES (continued)

The later in the NPI process an ECO is written, the greater its regular impact on the NPI schedule.

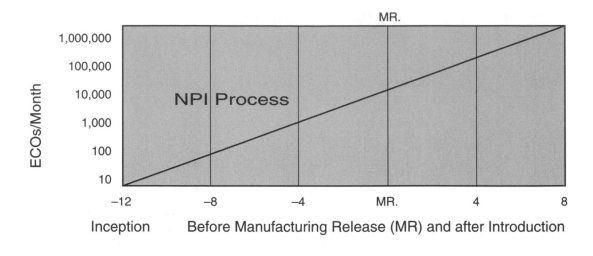

FIGURE 1-3. *Typical cost multiplier for design changes during the NPI process.*

_____

_____

_____

_____

_____

_____

EXERCISE 3:
Project Cost versus Project Schedule (Part III)

Summarize your recommendations and explain the trade-off.

_____

_____

_____

_____

QUESTIONS...

1. List the competitive issues that most affect your company.

_____

_____

_____

_____

_____

2. List five potential benefits of improving the NPI process.

_____

_____

_____

_____

_____

3. List and describe the major challenges facing businesses today.

_____

_____

_____

_____

_____

4. List three potential bottlenecks in making the NPI system work.

_____

_____

_____

_____

_____

. . . AND ANSWERS

1. Answers may vary based on individual company.

2. Increase in productivity
Reduction in costs
Reduction in product development times
Increase in product quality
Increase in profit over the product life cycle
Increase in customer satisfaction

3. Bringing information exchange systems and networks
Reducing costs
Delivering high-quality products through continuous process improvement
Being flexible and open to change
Developing an "informational" organization
Improving employee training and education
Improving information exchange systems and networks
Improving forecasting accuracy

4. Inflexible, "formal" organizational structures
Insufficiently trained and educated personnel
Inefficient informational systems
Accelerated flow of information and a demand to make well-informed decisions fast

M O D U L E

II

The Key Business Documents

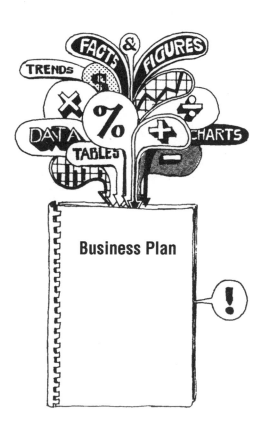

THE KEY BUSINESS DOCUMENTS

Companies today are under tremendous global pressure to reduce their product development times and costs without sacrificing quality. If you want to stay competitive and make a profit, you must bring your products to market faster, at lower cost, and with more value added. You must be flexible and open to change, and committed to improving your workforce through training and education. You must find better ways to communicate with your customers and suppliers and improve the accuracy of your forecasts. A well-documented NPI process plays a key role in meeting these challenges and helping you stay in business.

One of the prerequisites to making the NPI process work is the development of a series of key documents, including:

- A business plan and marketing strategy

- A marketing requirements document (MRD)

- An engineering requirements specification (ERS)

- A P&L statement

- A project plan

THE BUSINESS PLAN

The business plan is the key driver for the company. It articulates core company values and defines the company's mission. It creates a vision of what the company wants to be and delineates critical functional strategies—such as marketing, design (R&D), and manufacturing strategies of how to get there. Each of these strategies should include assumptions that are necessary to support the long-term sales portion of the business plan, and they should support a single company-wide plan while driving the NPI process.

Figure 2-1 lists the components of a business plan and shows how the long-term planning activities of the business plan drive key business strategies.

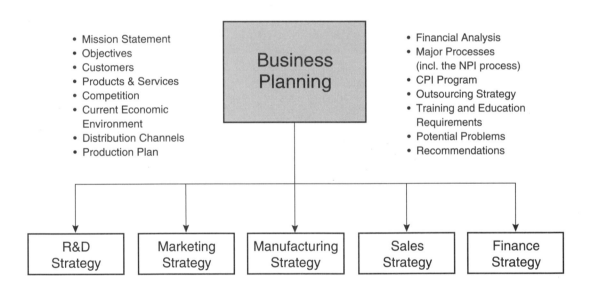

FIGURE 2-1. *The business planning/strategy interface.*

PREPARING THE MARKETING STRATEGY

The marketing strategy should support the business plan and the design (R&D) and manufacturing strategies. It may include answers to the following questions:

- What are the company's overall strategies?

- What market niches are being served?

- What products are being sold into those niches?

- What are the order winners and qualifiers for those products in those niches?

- What are the current and expected volumes and varieties for those products in each niche?

- What are the product-naming conventions?

The cornerstone of any marketing strategy is a single, company-wide product strategy that describes how, when, where, and against whom a company is going to compete. A company can compete on any of the following: price, quality, conformance (to the specs), perception (of the specs), delivery (speed and reliability), flexibility, product design (technology, features/options, and range), service (internal and external), and image.

When describing the competitive environment, it is important to identify the order winners, order qualifiers, and non-issues. Order winners are those characteristics the product has that customers prefer over the competitor's. Qualifiers are those characteristics that the product must have to even be considered by the customer. Non-issues are those characteristics that do not enter into the competitive picture. Care must be taken not to go with a perceived order winner that turns out to be a non-issue.

EXERCISE

In the space provided below, check off the order winners, order qualifiers, and non-issues that impact your company.

Competitive Issues	Order Qualifier	Order Winner	Non-Issue
Price			
Quality			
Conformance			
Perception			
Delivery			
Flexibility			
Product Design			
Service			
Image			

PREPARING THE MANUFACTURING STRATEGY

The manufacturing strategy should support the business plan and the marketing strategy. It may include:

- Dealing with long-term market trends

- Projected growth and variability of demand

- The emergence of new organizational structures

- The role of information technology

- The impact of capital investment in light of shorter product life cycles

- Key competitive measures, such as time to market, time to volume, time to profit, time to change, and quality

Another important component of the manufacturing strategy is a description of the plan to be used to manage each key supplier. This description should answer these questions:

- How are unique parts to be handled?

- What are the supplier-management objectives?

- What strategy will be used with each supplier to ensure that supplier-management objectives are met?

- What needs to be done with these key suppliers to support the marketing and design strategies, as well as the NPI process?

PREPARING THE DESIGN (R&D) STRATEGY

The R&D strategy details how a company develops products and technology for competitive advantage. There should only be a single, company-wide R&D strategy. It should support the business plan and the marketing strategy and address the following:

- Input from all appropriate internal functions, as well as customers and suppliers

- The technologies that the company needs to invest in

- How to obtain these technologies

- Technology road maps that describe the technology programs the company will invest in

- A technology integration plan that ensures that the selected technologies work well together

An effective technology integration process must be part of the earliest discussion of new products. If a company selects technologies that do not work well together, it can end up with a product that is hard to manufacture, late to market, and/or doesn't meet customer expectations. Marketing, and to a lesser extent Manufacturing (Operations) have to be extensively involved in the development of the R&D strategy to ensure that R&D projects are market focused and manufacturable.

THE MARKET REQUIREMENTS DOCUMENT

The major purpose of the market requirements document (MRD) is to establish an agreement between the members of the NPI team, executives, key suppliers, and customers. In it, you should address questions such as:

- Who are the customers?

- How does this product fit into the company's product family and overall business strategy?

- What problem(s) is the product going to solve?

- What are the product requirements (features, advantages, and benefits)?

- Who is the competition?

- What is unique about this product when compared to the competition?

- What is the projected revenue and profit potential?

- What are the globalization issues?

- What are the supply issues?

One of the major causes of NPI schedule delays is the lack of detail in the MRD. The customer survey portion of the MRD should inform the NPI team members of how target customers perceive and deal with unfulfilled needs using existing products and/or technologies. This helps them to determine new product features, advantages, and benefits. In general, make the MRD writing process an interactive one. The more cross-functional feedback the better. At this stage, you want innovative ideas flowing from the executives, operations, marketing, customers, and strategic suppliers.

In summary, an MRD should be brief and to the point. It should describe the customer needs, the product that is going to satisfy those needs, a statement of the expected financial benefits, and finally, how the product fits into the overall marketing and R&D strategies, as well as the business plan. This should include a recommendation to move forward or cancel the project. Remember, a well-written MRD ensures early executive buy-in and avoids disagreement later.

Sample Questions for the Customer Survey

Following is a list of questions which could be the basis for developing a customer survey. Under each major question are additional questions that should be considered in answering the major questions.

1. How does the project fit into the overall product family and business strategy?

   a) Describe how the product fits with the marketing strategy.

   b) Describe how the product fits with the R&D strategy.

   c) Describe how the product fits with the business plan.

2. What problems does this product solve?

   a) What is the customer willing to pay for?

   b) What is the market research process?

   c) What were the results of the survey?

   d) What are the trends?

3. What are the key product requirements?

   a) What does the product look like?

   b) What are the features, advantages, and benefits?

   c) What are the assumptions?

   d) What is the market place?

   e) How will this product be different than others?

   f) How will the product be packaged?

   g) How will the product be distributed?

   h) What is the migration path?

4. Who are the customers?

   a) Who are the target customers?

   b) What is the geographic location of these customers (domestic, international, and so on)?

   c) Are there any unique requirements (international, etc.)?

   d) What will the channel of distribution look like?

5. What is the competitive situation?

   a) Who are the competitors, and what is their market share?

   b) What are the key competitive advantages (solutions) of this product?

   c) What are the trends?

   d) What is the window of opportunity?

   e) What are the order winners?

   f) What are the order qualifiers?

   g) What are the international issues, if any?

6. How would you describe the technology integration process?

   a) What new technologies are being introduced?

THE ENGINEERING REQUIREMENTS SPECIFICATION

The engineering requirements specification (ERS) should take into account the product features and advantages listed in the MRD, and include all critical engineering parameters that define the functionality requirements of the product. It may also refer to corporate specs for emissions, agency compliance, environmental conditions, packaging, cosmetic quality, and others. In addition, the ERS can comment on the:

- Requirements for common parts
- Requirements for unique parts with justification
- Software specification (if appropriate)
- Reliability plan
- Capacity of the R&D organization
- New pro forma profit and loss statement
- Options

A crucial part of the engineering requirement specifications is the bill of materials (BOM). The BOM is a list of parts and quantities that go into the end product. The objective is to identify cost savings and achieve 100 percent accuracy as soon as possible. At this point, Documentation Control should be involved in educating engineers on how the system works, and suggesting ways to avoid administrative waste. The BOM represents the estimate of what the assemblies' subassemblies (make) and purchased parts will be. Every effort should be made to determine:

- The costs, including mutual costs for common parts as well as unique parts
- The cost of direct labor, as well as factory overhead
- The percentage of common parts

The ERS is required in order to prepare a request for quote, and enables suppliers to respond to these requirements.

One way to bring products to market at a reduced cost and increased profit margin is to strive for commonality of parts. For parts that are neither finalized nor defined, the concept of placeholders should be used. This concept allows for lower-level planning to continue while the part design is being finalized. Be sure to replace the placeholders when the BOM is updated in order to avoid having the wrong part purchased or made.

THE PRO FORMA PROFIT AND LOSS STATEMENT

It is never too early to begin projecting the potential financial benefits for the company. The project manager should develop a pro forma profit and loss (P&L) state-ment, including targeted ROIs and ROAs. The question to be answered is, "Should the company continue to invest in the project?" These projections must be updated during the NPI process and reviewed in detail throughout the product life cycle. Measurements are meant to:

- Establish the basis for corrective action (on an ongoing basis)

- Measure performance

- Establish the basis for improvement

- Provide the basis for communicating progress

- Answer the questions, "Are we on budget? Are we on time?"

In addition to the financial measures, the following nonfinancial measures should be considered:

- Market share, product availability, backlog levels

- Team work

- Customer satisfaction

- Percentage of customer requirements in the final product

- Number of customer requirements/number of unique parts

In summary, use only a few selected measures. Too many measurements will kill a project; too few will render it rudderless. Focus on the customer's perception of value, and take the time to collect good data, and then objectively analyze the information the data provides. There are very few measurements people really care about.

ACTION

Review the following P&L statement and indicate how revenue can be increased and cost can be decreased.

Item	YEAR 1 Amt.	YEAR 1 % of Cost	YEAR N+2 Amt.	YEAR N+2 % of Cost
Total Revenue Year (Domestic & International)				
Cost of Goods Sold				
Direct Material				
Less Scrap or Salvage				
Net Direct Material				
Subcontractor's Process/Services Utilized				
Direct Labor Hours at $				
Factory Overhead				
(a) Tools and Dies				
(b) Indirect Materials				
(c) Indirect Factory Expenses (State Basis of Allocation)				
(d) Miscellaneous				
(e) Engineering and Development Expenses—direct				
(1) Salaries and Wages				
(2) Design Tools and Software				
(3) Other				
Total Manufacturing Cost				
General Selling and Administrative Expense:				
Percent of				
Profit				
Cost of Field Service (Transportation, Parts, Time)				
Cost of Handling/Coordinating				
Cost of Rework				
Cost of Customer Dissatisfaction				
Cost of Future ECOs				
Cost of Product Liability				
Cost of Management				

Product Life Cycle

THE PROJECT PLAN

The project plan is the responsibility of the project manager and should include sections from the MRD such as the customer survey, pricing, product features, and so on. It should identify the roles and responsibilities of the individual NPI team members during each phase of the NPI process, and contain a standard list of tasks and *estimated* timelines for the completion of each task. (*Note:* Providing these estimates is a major prerequisite to success, since it enables the project manager to establish realistic completion dates. At a minimum, the plan should have estimated dates at weekly levels.) It is vital to the success of the new project development effort that the key team members agree on the contents of this plan, the schedule, and the roles and responsibilities of the team members.

The project plan is finalized at the end of the second phase of the NPI process, the investigation phase, and then updated as the project moves along by the project leader with the help of the NPI team. Each functional area covered in the plan is prepared and/or reviewed by the team representative for that function. For example, Finance prepares the unit cost analysis, R&D reviews the testing time allotted in the schedule, and Marketing provides input regarding the product transition plan, which details the transition from R&D to manufacturing and the end customer, and complements the project plan.

Following is a summary of additional considerations when developing a project plan:

- Make sure there are measurable, attainable, and observable objectives. These objectives should describe how they support the business plan and the appropriate functional strategies.

- To the extent possible, describe the scope of the project as well as a short narrative on what success will look like.

- Describe your customers, both internal and external. List the stakeholders responsible for the final decisions. Also describe how out-of-bound items will be communicated.

- Provide a technical assessment (including technical risks) and describe the key features and added-value features of the product. Identify any features contained in the MRD that cannot be incorporated into the product.

- Describe the key tasks, time estimates, and responsibilities. The key tasks and estimated timelines must be supported with unit cost estimates and budgets, as well as any special resource requirements, including outside experts, consultants, and so on.

QUESTIONS . . .

1. List five components of a business plan.

_____

_____

_____

_____

_____

2. List five questions that should be answered when developing a marketing strategy.

_____

_____

_____

_____

_____

3. List five components of a manufacturing strategy.

_____

_____

_____

_____

_____

4. List five questions the marketing requirements document should answer.

_____

_____

_____

_____

_____

5. Define the design (R&D) strategy.

_____

_____

_____

_____

_____

_____

...AND ANSWERS

1. Mission statement
   Objectives
   Customers
   Competition
   R&D, marketing, and manufacturing strategies
   Current economic environment
   Distribution channels
   Production/sales and operation plan (including the resource plan)
   Financial analysis
   Major processes
   Continuous process improvement program
   Training and education strategy
   Potential problems
   Recommendations and plan of action to implement them

2. What are the company's overall strategies?
   What market niches are being served?
   What products are being sold into those niches?
   What are the order winners and qualifiers for those products in those niches?
   What are the current and expected volumes and varieties for those products in each niche?

3. Dealing with long-term market trends
   Projected growth and variability of demand
   The emergence of new technologies
   The emergence of new organization structures
   The role of information technology
   The impact of capital investment in light of shorter product life cycles
   Key competitive issues, such as time to market, time to volume, time to profit, time to change, and quality

   Another important component of the manufacturing strategy is a description of the plan to be used for managing each supplier. This description should answer these questions:

   What are the supplier-management objectives?

What strategy will be used with each supplier to ensure that supplier-management objectives are met?

What needs to be done to support the marketing and R&D strategies, and the NPI process?

4. Who are the customers?

How does this product fit into the company's product family strategy and the overall business strategy?

What problem(s) is the product going to solve?

What are the product requirements (features, advantages, and benefits)?

Who is the competition?

What is the projected revenue and profit potential?

What are the globalization issues?

What are the supply issues?

5. The R&D strategy details how a company develops products and technology for competitive advantage. There should only be a single, company-wide R&D strategy. It should support the business plan and the marketing strategy and address the following:

Input from all appropriate internal functions, as well as customers and suppliers

The technologies that the company needs to invest in

How to obtain these technologies

Technology road maps that describe the technology programs the company will invest in

A technology integration plan that ensures that the selected technologies work well together

MODULE

III

Changing the
Organizational
Structures

THE EMERGING INFORMATION ORGANIZATION

The organizational structures within companies will have to change radically in order to support an increasing number of products with increasingly shorter product life cycles. Incremental change is not enough. Organizations must be able to renew and reinvent themselves. Team-based organizations are the basic building blocks for these organizations to be successful.

To increase an organization's ability to bring products to market faster, employees need to be trained and educated in all facets of the NPI process, including business and financial matters, continuous process improvement, and team work. People must understand the reason the company is in business. This purpose must be communicated through the business plan. People must understand the challenges as well as the competitive pressures the company is faced with. The executive team likewise must understand the challenges and pressures its people are faced with. People must understand how they fit in, how they will share in the gains, and why change is good for them and the company. As was stated earlier, there will be at least two organizational structures in every company—a traditional formal organization and an emerging informational organization.

This module presents the role of the information organization as an emerging structure and tool that integrates suppliers as well as customers into an interconnected series of organizational structures, all dedicated to bringing products to market faster, and supporting the NPI process.

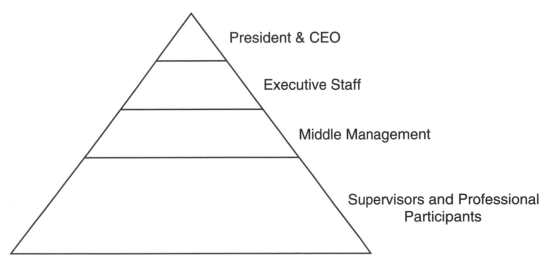

FIGURE 3-1. *A typical hierarchical organization.*

THE EMERGING INFORMATION ORGANIZATION (continued)

Figure 3-1 shows the traditional hierarchical organization. List how this typical organization could impact the NPI process.

_____

_____

_____

_____

_____

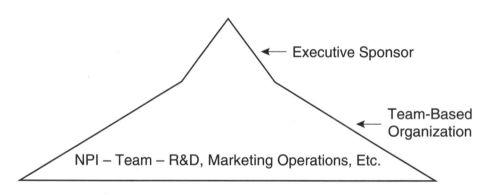

FIGURE 3-2. *The emerging informational organization.*

Figure 3-2 shows the emerging informational organization that represents the environment of the NPI team. List the benefits of this team-based organization. What are the consequences if this alternative organization is integrated into a company's traditional hierarchical organization?

_____

_____

_____

_____

_____

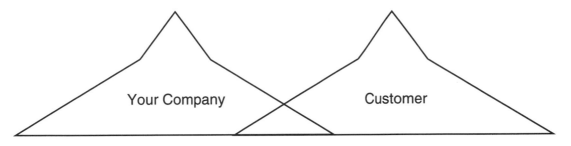

FIGURE 3-3. *Team-based organization linked to the customer.*

Figure 3-3 links the team-based organization to the customer to develop an early involvement process in the beginning of the supply chain management. List the benefits of this extended organization.

_____

_____

_____

_____

_____

_____

_____

_____

_____

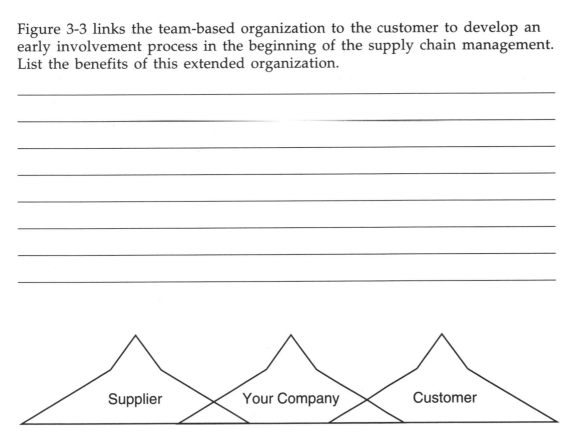

FIGURE 3-4. *Team-based organization linked to the customer and supplier.*

THE EMERGING INFORMATION ORGANIZATION (continued)

In Figure 3-4, the chain is expanded to include the supplier. List the benefits of this further expansion of the NPI team-based organization.

_____

_____

_____

_____

_____

To sustain the flow of information between the major players in this emerging system, companies must develop and implement more advanced information exchange systems and networks. The end result will be the extended enterprise as shown in Figure 3-5.

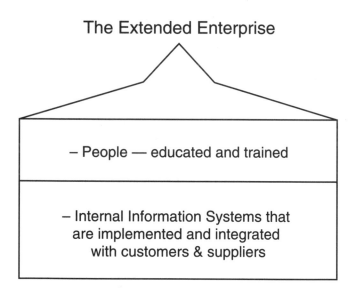

FIGURE 3-5. *The extended enterprise.*

Potentially, the continuous flow of information to and from customers and key suppliers can reduce both time to market and costs, thus increasing profit margins and market share. This approach is not only being embraced by Internet and software companies, but also by the automotive, aircraft, and computer industries to name just a few.

THE SELECTION OF TEAM MEMBERS

One of the major success factors in the introduction of a new product is the team that is assembled to bring it to market. The selection and subsequent training of the team members is essential for success, and should be looked up to as a documented process. This process starts with (1) an assessment of the current organization, and (2) a search for self-directed people that can be trained to work as a team to achieve its stated objectives.

In order for this to happen quickly and efficiently, organizational changes need to take place that allow for self-directed teams, which—when reaching critical mass—become a self-directed organization. There must be an environment in which it is safe for people to make errors, and then *learn* from them. (*Note:* This does NOT grant a license to make the same error over and over—common sense must prevail.) However, before people can become empowered decision-makers, they must be trained in how to identify problems, determine what the best potential solution is, and then make a well-informed decision. Employees at all levels need to be *involved* over a period of time in the decision-making process so they can develop empowered decision-making skills.

Companies today are spending a tremendous amount of time evaluating what skills their workforce has and what skills the workforce will need during the coming years. Figure 3-6 shows this process, called a GAPP analysis.

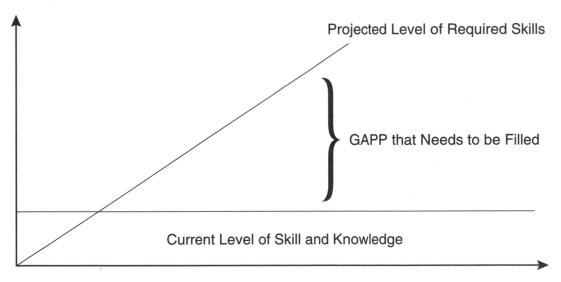

FIGURE 3-6. *The GAPP analysis determines the current and required skills of the workforce.*

THE SELECTION OF TEAM MEMBERS (continued)

The first step in performing a GAPP analysis is to list the skills required to access the current levels of skills and knowledge within the organization. Extensive company-wide needs assessments and GAPP analysis can be done at great expenditures of time and money. Many companies today are performing these analyses for specific functions (such as procurement) or specific teams (such as NPI teams) and are having quick successes.

Next, make a list of the skills and knowledge of your workforce and break it down into the skills and knowledge that are directly related to the business. A second cut at this list of skills and knowledge is a distinction between "hard" skills and "soft" skills. Technical "hard" skills are defined as the skills and knowledge that are directly related to business activities and that support the NPI process. "Soft" skills are defined as the skills and knowledge used to facilitate and support the execution of activities related to the NPI process (i.e., people skills).

Prior to ever being selected for a team, a curriculum should be set up that provides training for potential team members. The time to train people is prior to their selection and participation in the NPI team. The training and human resource departments should be actively involved in the development of the selection process for NPI team members.

Here is the skeleton of a basic curriculum, which should be customized to fit an individual company situation:

► **Project Management**

► **Basics of New Product Introduction**

► **Time Management**

► **Meeting Management**

► **Continuous Process Improvement & Related Quality Tools**

► **Basics of Finance**

► **Team Training**

Many of these topics can be covered briefly in the first meeting of the NPI team. For example, meeting management can be as brief as simply reviewing a list of standardized rules and making modifications to fit the environment.

In addition to the basic curriculum, a technical curriculum should be developed for each of the functional areas. Following is an example of how one company developed a standard list of "meeting norms."

Meeting Norms

- Visible action list is to be kept

- Be tough on covering agenda items and on timing, or renegotiate time as a group

- No "ins and outs"

- Confidentiality is to be maintained

- Put breaks on agenda

- All "one-on-ones" are to be handled outside committee

- Agenda content: Nothing that can be sent out or read should be covered in the meeting

- Process for getting items on agenda:
  —Proposed by anyone
  —Identify topic owner
  —State expected outcome
  —State time required
  —Keep running list of agenda topics for the remainder of the year (Meeting Map)
  —Draft agenda for next meeting at the end of each meeting
  —Prepublish agendas
  —Minimize open-ended discussions
  —Come to some closure—force decisions

THE BASICS OF PROJECT MANAGEMENT

One of the most important areas to be included in the NPI team training curriculum is good project management. This should be simple to use and understand, and at a minimum cover the following project management and scheduling tools:

- Project time table with tasks for each phase (Gantt chart)

- Rules for running meetings and a method for recording the results of the meeting

- Decision logs with a running list of changes in the original MRD, ERS, and project plan

- A boilerplate for letters and reports, including the customer survey, the project initiation letter, and so on. Use your technical writing department to help out here.

Potential project managers should be trained in the use of various project management tools such as:

- The project plan (see earlier in this module)

- The communication plan, which describes how meetings will be set up, decisions communicated, and success measured

- A supporting document that includes a column for time estimates as well as a column for actual time spent called "Detailed Tasks/Time Estimates"

- A Gantt chart to which the project manager applies the totaled estimated times

- A decision log, used to record key decisions that impact the direction, objectives, cost, or due dates of a project

- A mechanism for identifying the slipped due dates or substantial cost overruns

Estimated Time/Capacity						
Project Name: _____			*Scope:* _____			
What: (objective)			Budget:			
Why:			Approval:			
Tasks	Assumptions	Estimated Time	Actual Time	Major Differences	Explanation of Corrective Action	Responsibilities

The Detailed Task/Time Estimates Support Document

THE BASICS OF PROJECT MANAGEMENT
(continued)

The Time-Phased Approach										
	Phase I			Phase II			Phase III			
Task(s)	J	F	M	A	M	J	J	A	S	O
(Est. hrs.)										
Vacations										
Time out										
Totals										

The Gantt chart—a time-phased approach to project management

To:	Executive Sponsor		
From:	Project Manager		
CC:	All NPI Team Members		
Date:	Decision #		Description (of the impact of the decision on costs, features, time schedule, functionality, etc.)

The decision log—one of the most effective tools in documenting the decision process that leads to results. It also records valuable information in terms of improving future projects.

Schedule	Actual	Budget	Description	Corrective Action
Dates				
Cost				
Other				

Simple reports like this one above should be used to highlight when previously agreed-to dates slip or costs exceed the budget, and an appropriate corrective action should be noted.

OTHER PROJECT SCHEDULING TOOLS

Scheduling build-to-order, or custom types of engineered-to-order products, presents some special types of project scheduling issues. The reason for the challenge is that a longer planning horizon expands capacity needs, and because of the very complex R&D, production, and material planning and scheduling issues.

To address these issues, a method called critical path method (CPM) or a variation called program evaluation and review techniques (PERT) is used.

These project management tools lay the task out in a network. The routing for the new product could be the network. Times (lead times) are estimated for each task. This network or routing is analyzed to identify what is called the critical path or the longest lead time path.

The estimates of time for each step are then monitored and updated. Any problems are identified, and corrective action is taken.

M O D U L E

IV

The Major Phases of the New Product Introduction Process

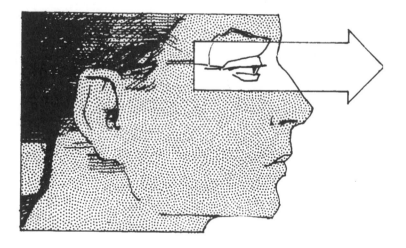

THE NEW PRODUCT INTRODUCTION PROCESS

A large number of companies divide their NPI processes into a series of standardized phases (aka "gates") that have well-defined beginning and ending points and measurable criteria for successful completion. As mentioned before, this detailed breakdown enables the NPI team leader or project manager to monitor progress against pre-established goals.

At the completion of each phase, the project manager conducts phase review meetings that are attended by NPI team members, as well as the executive sponsor. The purpose of these meetings is to identify the scope and nature of potential problems and passing responsibility for resolution. In general, the agenda of these phase review meetings deals with the NPI process and scheduled dates, as well as with strategic technical, financial, quality, and market-driven concerns. In addition, the participants in these meetings address concerns such as program continuation, changes in scope, and timing.

Here is a list of the various phases in order of progression:

PHASE 1: The concept phase

PHASE 2: The investigation phase

PHASE 3: The design (R&D) phase

PHASE 4: The manufacturability phase

PHASE 5: The introduction phase

PHASE 6: The product transition and postmortem phase

Traditionally, companies have approached this process sequentially, completing one phase then moving on to the next one (see Figure 4-1). Today's business challenges, however, have forced companies to switch to a more flexible NPI process that allows for parallel efforts and changes to take place up to the last minute and at minimum cost (see Figure 4-2).

THE NEW PRODUCT INTRODUCTION PROCESS (continued)

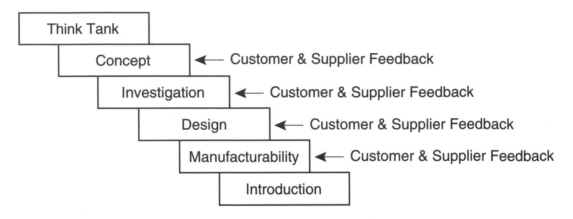

FIGURE 4-1. *The traditional NPI process.*

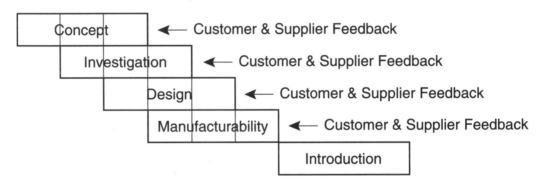

FIGURE 4-2. *The improved, more flexible NPI process.*

A major prerequisite for this type of NPI process to work is the development and deployment of an information exchange system that guarantees a continuous flow of information to and from customers and key suppliers and grants internal team members unlimited access to the new product development efforts. The use of the Internet and the development of web sites already provides a solution to this information bottleneck. You can yield even better results if you succeed in integrating the company's manufacturing systems, such as Manufacturing Resource Planning (MRPII) or its expanded version called Enterprise Resource Planning (ERP), with the engineering software packages, as well as the MRPII systems of your customers and key suppliers (see Figure 4-3). Remember, the earlier you involve key suppliers and customers in the new product development efforts, the better your chances of shortening your product introduction cycles.

The remainder of this module presents an overview of each phase of the NPI process. It describes the major tasks and identifies the roles and responsibilities of the NPI team members. At the end of this module, you will be given the opportunity to review a list of roles and responsibilities for each phase of the NPI process. These lists, while by no means comprehensive, are intended to be used as "thought starters" for more comprehensive lists that can be used to customize your company's NPI process.

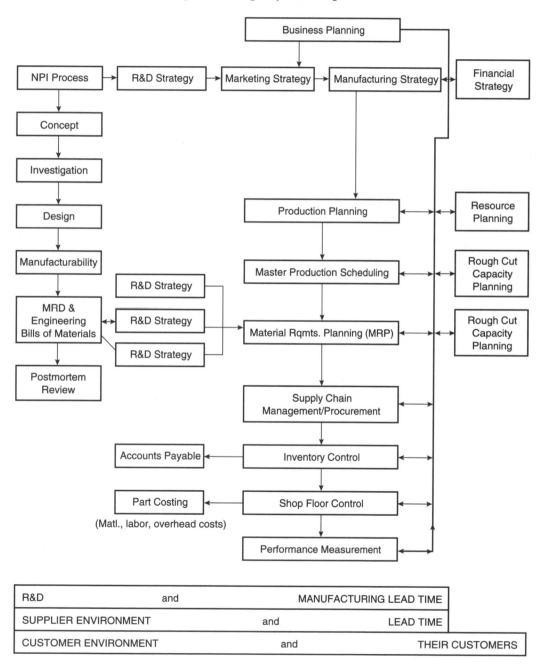

FIGURE 4-3. *The interface betweeen NPI process and MRPII.*

THE CONCEPT PHASE

During the concept phase, the decision to look at the possibility of bringing a product to market is made. The decision is a formal one, pending approval by the executive sponsor and other members of the executive team who look at the product's market potential and its contribution to the overall goals of the company. The proposed program may vary in size, depending on whether it is primarily on the integration of existing product designs or whether it involves largely new designs.

If the product development is to go forward, the executives approve funding for the next stage in the NPI process, the investigation phase, and ensure that the new product proposal is in alignment with the corporate business plan, the key corporate strategies, and the other projects that are under way or being planned.

To aid in this decision-making process, the product marketing group prepares the market requirements document (MRD), the project manager develops the preliminary project plan, and the R&D group drafts the preliminary engineering requirements specification (ERS). (For more details on the MRD, ERS, and project plan, see Module II.) In summary, these documents will have to address these questions:

- Is the product feasible?

- Is it in alignment with the corporate product strategy?

- Has the "Voice of the Customer" and the "Voice of the Supplier" exercise supported the decision to proceed with the product?

- Has a projected return on investment (ROI) and return on asset (ROA) calculation been completed? Are these measurements supported by pro forma P&L statements?

- Is there a first-pass written description that defines the roles and responsibilities of the NPI team members?

- Have all functions been included in these early stages? (Remember, the product life cycle will be locked in even at this point.)

THE INVESTIGATION PHASE

This critical phase establishes the parameters of the new product development effort. To ensure that the new product meets or exceeds customer expectations, Marketing tests the "voice of the customer" by conducting customer surveys, running focus groups, and utilizing tools such as affinity diagrams and quality function deployment (QDF).

The major objective of the investigation phase is to translate customer needs as outlined in the market requirements document (MRD) into detailed technical requirements for purchased item assemblies up through the end item. Financial considerations such as pricing, return on assets, and return on investments are updated, and major costs of people, equipment, and materials must be estimated. These initial costs should also set targets for reducing the number of engineering change orders (ECOs).

The procurement/supply-based management members should submit a material requirements plan that includes cost avoidance as well as cost reduction strategies over the life of the project. Long lead time items should be identified and negotiations started with the key suppliers. Manufacturing engineers should provide modifications to the existing processes and identify new ones. New equipment acquisition budgets must be prepared, and given to the capital equipment buyer. The earlier the appropriate procurement persons become involved, the more time they have to develop their selection and negotiation strategies. This is particularly critical in the case of new and unique parts.

The customer service and support group should submit an initial support plan and continue to solicit feedback from key customers through customer focus groups. Globalization and localization strategies must be addressed, and the preliminary product transition plan must be completed and added to the project plan.

Finally, an updated, detailed project plan, complete with engineering specifications, is submitted for approval. Once management has approved the project funding and allocated the required resources, the project leader finalizes the estimated timelines and, with the help of the project team, updates the detailed task list for each phase with the functional roles and responsibilities spelled out. Remember, these tasks and time estimates provide the basis for developing standard tasks and time frames for the NPI process, now and in the future.

The investigation phase typically begins about half way through the concept phase, and continues until after its completion.

THE DESIGN (R&D) PHASE

Once the project plan has been approved, R&D can begin with the actual product design and update the initial product specifications, schedules, and the first draft of the bill of materials (BOM) list.

The major objective of this phase is to prove the integrity of the design. The second objective is to test the manufacturing processes by producing units in a production environment.

Reliability plans are developed with preliminary goals and objectives established. For products sold globally, location plans are finalized. Documentation is produced that will communicate the design concept to the various functional groups for their review, planning, and feedback. Prototypes are built and tested in non-customer facilities (aka alpha testing) to demonstrate the soundness of the basic design approach. The availability of parts is verified, and manuals and other documentation are available for "first pass" review. (Many companies are starting to include the technical writers, who produce "boiler plate" product documentation earlier and earlier in the process.) At this point, the product may be tested in potential customer facilities (aka beta testing). If software is part of the product, the code is reviewed and final testing and acceptance is well under way.

During the design phase, functional workloads start to increase. Marketing must include the forecast assumptions in the forecasting model. This is the time to review prior product forecasts, consult the sales force, and update the projected market potential for this product. At this point, the technical publications arm of the marketing department is producing drafts of manuals to be used in the beta testing process.

Manufacturing starts to test new or existing production processes, to ensure they are ready to accept the volume required. The material contracts are finalized. When unique parts are being considered, suppliers must be qualified and certified. Contract negotiation, process reviews, and financial evaluation of potential suppliers are conducted. The rules and disciplines of the BOMs are established, and the final cost, price, and marketing numbers are entered into the appropriate information system. All risk buys (unique parts) should be completed at this point.

Service and support groups are chartered with gathering detailed customer feedback. The warranty model is completed, along with the final field service plan and all technical documentation. The first part of a warranty expense model is constructed and tested. Service requirements for the suppliers providing parts are also developed.

In the meantime, the project manager must make sure that Legal has signed off on any issues regarding patents, copyrights, and so on.

The main questions to be asked, answered, and updated throughout this phase are:

- Are we on schedule?

- Are we on budget?

- Can we make what the customer is asking for?

- Are they willing to pay the price, and will it give us the profit we're looking for?

Before the end of this phase, the approved project plan from the investigation phase must be reviewed and updated. The updating includes schedule refinements, cost updates, and so on. The design phase is essentially complete when the alpha review has been conducted, and all product drawings and department "key plans" are released.

THE MANUFACTURABILITY PHASE

The manufacturability phase has two objectives: (1) to determine the capability to plan, buy, build, test, install, and service the product, based on the engineering BOM; and (2) to evaluate new product performance (including technical performance, reliability, and service) and customer satisfaction at the customer site.

A key part of the manufacturability phase is the production ramp phase. Its purpose is not only to evaluate the proposed new product from a business standpoint, but to evaluate pending ECOs. Failure to do this results in too many ECOs after the product has been introduced. The cost as well as the responsibility needs to be clearly defined so the trade-off between time to market and cost reduction can be made. The bottom line is that these potential costs must be included in the product cost and not become part of the hidden cost of manufacturing, and consequently contribute to profit erosion.

At this point, the NPI team members and manager should ask themselves, does it really make sense to undertake sustained production of the proposed product from a business and financial viewpoint? If so, then full-scale production (aka ramp) is approved. If not, they need to identify specific action items that are necessary to resolve these key issues. When a predetermined production rate (defined in the program plan) is achieved, and plans to resolve the outstanding issues are substantively under way and approved at the phase review meeting, the production ramp of the manufacturability phase is well on its way to completion.

In summary, the basic design of the product is tested during the design phase. The level of customer satisfaction and the ability to build the new product in volume is tested during the manufacturability phase. The manufacturability phase is considered complete when the two objectives listed above have been accomplished.

THE INTRODUCTION PHASE

The introduction phase is intended to produce products, generate revenue, and to ship to the customer when promised. Its major objectives are:

- To be able to produce the product in volume per the target cost model, and satisfy customer demand

- To respond to customer problems

- To meet the revenue projections

- To meet and exceed customer expectations

THE PRODUCT TRANSITION AND POSTMORTEM PHASE

There must be a well thought-out and executed product transition and a well-documented postmortem that covers what happens up to and including the official product introduction, and what the plans are in going forward.

The product transition is the responsibility of the project leader and the product marketing manager, who both stay with the product for six months, or until manufacturing and the sustaining project manager agree all major issues with the product have been resolved. This at least reduces the emotionality of releasing products before they are really ready, just to meet marketing release (MR) dates. It also establishes a mechanism for collecting additional financial data (such as number and cost of ECOs) and for continuing to track the product life cycle P&Ls.

In order to facilitate the product transition, schedule a series of postmortem meetings over the next three to nine months. The purpose of these meetings is to evaluate the NPI process (What did/did not work? What needs improvement/should be discarded?), facilitate the learning experience, and fine-tune the P&L over the product life cycle.

Following is a list of postmortem topics that should be addressed in a series of meetings:

- Review and update of "survey questions" (Most companies do not do this, and if they do they wait until the end.)

- Review of ECOs and their related cost (tie to performance measure)

- Review of cost/projected revenue for the next six months (tie to the performance measure)

- Review of major issues that impacted the NPI, establishment of root causes, and when appropriate, adjustments to the company's formal NPI process

- Rewards and recognition meetings (Executive sponsors and CEO should chair these meetings)

EXERCISES

In the following exercises the concepts covered in the description of each of the phases will be reviewed. The following rules and responsibilities exercises can be done in groups or individually. The answers follow each exercise.

Exercises—Roles and Responsibilities

EXERCISE 1:
The Concept Phase—Roles and Responsibilities

Instructions: Indicate in the table below who is responsible for each task. (For example, in the first row (customer survey) under project manager (PM) it lists "KP" for key participant and under marketing department (M) it lists "R" for responsible.) In the blank lines at the bottom you can list tasks that are specific to your company or project.

Tasks	PM	M	R&D	O	ME	E	CS	Other
Develop Customer Survey (Tie to MRD)	KP	R						
Develop Project Plan								
Develop ERS/Technical Plan (Tie to Customer Survey)								
Select Team Members								
Select Phase Review Board								
Write Program Initiation Letter								
Identify the NPI and Other Processes								
Develop Pro Forma P&L, Cost Tracking over Product Life Cycle, Incentive Plan								
Define External Training								
Define Internal Training								
Determine Make/Buy Decisions								
Establish Teaming/Partnering Agreement								
Review Legal Issues (Copyrights, Patents, Non-Disclosures)								
Hold Program Kick-off								
Hold Phase Review Meeting								
Identify Sustaining Product Manager								

Functional Description		Responsibility	
PM	Project Manager	R	Responsible
M	Marketing	KP	Key Participant
R&D	Research & Development (Design Engineer)	A	Attend or Participate
O	Operations (Doc Control Purchasing, Materials, Proclamation, and so on)		
ME	Manufacturing Engineers		
E	Executive Sponsor		
CS	Customer Support		
Other	Legal, Finance, Quality		

KEY TO EXERCISE 1:
The Concept Phase—Roles and Responsibilities

Note: The suggested answers represent a summary of several different companies and may vary from company to company. The task list is by no means comprehensive, and should be customized to fit your company's environment.

Tasks	PM	M	R&D	O	ME	E	CS	Other
Develop Customer Survey (Tie to MRD)	KP	R	KP	KP				
Develop Project Plan	R							
Develop ERS/Technical Plan (Tie to Customer Survey)	KP		R					
Select Team Members	KP	KP	KP	A	A	R	A	A
Select Phase Review Board								
Write Program Initiation Letter	KP					R		
Identify the NPI and Other Processes	R		KP	KP	KP			
Develop Pro Forma P&L, Cost Tracking over Product Life Cycle, Incentive Plan	R	KP	KP	KP			A	KP
Define External Training	KP	R	KP	KP				
Define Internal Training	KP		KP	R	KP			
Determine Make/Buy Decisions	KP	KP	KP	R	KP			
Establish Teaming/Partnering Agreement	KP			R				
Review Legal Issues (Copyrights, Patents, Non-Disclosures)	KP							R
Hold Program Kick-off	R	A	A	A	A	A	A	A
Hold Phase Review Meeting	KP	R	KP	KP		KP	KP	
Identify Sustaining Product Manager	R	A	A	A	A	A	A	A

Functional Description		Responsibility	
PM	Project Manager	R	Responsible
M	Marketing	KP	Key Participant
R&D	Research & Development (Design Engineer)	A	Attend or Participate
O	Operations (Doc Control Purchasing, Materials, Proclamation, and so on)		
ME	Manufacturing Engineers		
E	Executive Sponsor		
CS	Customer Support		
Other	Legal, Finance, Quality		

EXERCISE 2:
The Investigation Phase—Roles and Responsibilities

Instructions: Indicate in the table below who is responsible for each task and who are the key participants and attendees. In the blank lines at the bottom you can list tasks that are specific to your company or project.

Tasks	PM	M	R&D	O	ME	E	CS	Other
Release Requirement Plans								
Assemblies								
Sub-Assemblies								
Purchased								
Software								
Other								
Release Product Development Plans								
Hardware								
Software								
Release Reliability Plan								
Review Manufacturing Plan								
Review Manufacturing Engineering Plan								
Review Documentation Plan								
Review QA Plan								
Review Agency Plan								
Review Alpha- and Beta-Testing Plans								
Review Product Structure								
Product Transition Plan								
Hold Phase Review Meeting								

Functional Description		Responsibility	
PM	Project Manager	R	Responsible
M	Marketing	KP	Key Participant
R&D	Research & Development (Design Engineer)	A	Attend or Participate
O	Operations (Doc Control Purchasing, Materials, Proclamation, and so on)		
ME	Manufacturing Engineers		
E	Executive Sponsor		
CS	Customer Support		
Other	Legal, Finance, Quality		

KEY TO EXERCISE 2:
The Investigation Phase—Roles and Responsibilities

Note: The suggested answers represent a summary of several different companies and may vary from company to company. The task list is by no means comprehensive, and should be customized to fit your company's environment.

Tasks	PM	M	R&D	O	ME	E	CS	Other
Release Requirement Plans								
Assemblies	KP	A	R	KP	KP			
Sub-Assemblies	KP	A	R	KP	KP			
Purchased	KP	A	R	KP				
Software	KP	A	R	KP				
Other								
Release Product Development Plans								
Hardware	KP		R					
Software	KP		R					
Release Reliability Plan	KP		R					
Review Manufacturing Plan	KP			R				
Review Manufacturing Engineering Plan	KP				R			
Review Documentation Plan	KP		KP	R				
Review QA Plan		KP		KP				R
Review Agency Plan	KP	KP	KP					R
Review Alpha- and Beta-Testing Plans	KP	KP	R					KP
Review Product Structure	KP		R	KP				
Product Transition Plan	KP	R	KP	KP	A	KP	A	R
Hold Phase Review Meeting	R	KP	KP	KP	KP	A	A	

Functional Description		Responsibility	
PM	Project Manager	R	Responsible
M	Marketing	KP	Key Participant
R&D	Research & Development (Design Engineer)	A	Attend or Participate
O	Operations (Doc Control Purchasing, Materials, Proclamation, and so on)		
ME	Manufacturing Engineers		
E	Executive Sponsor		
CS	Customer Support		
Other	Legal, Finance, Quality		

EXERCISE 3:
The Design Phase—Roles and Responsibilities

Instructions: Indicate in the table below who is responsible for each task and who are the key participants and attendees. In the blank lines at the bottom you can list tasks that are specific to your company or project.

Tasks	PM	M	R&D	O	ME	E	CS	Other
Hold Design Reviews for								
Assemblies								
Sub-Assemblies								
Purchased Parts								
Software								
Other								
Track Progression on all Key Plans (MFG, QA, ME, etc.)								
Sign Alpha and Beta Site Agreement								
Release Product Drawings								
Release Assemblies and Sub-Assemblies								
Release Software								
Complete Alpha Test								
Update Engineering Bill of Materials								
Create Planning Bill of Materials								
Finalize Training Plans								
Update Approved Vendor List (AVL)								
Update Pro Forma P&L								
Confirm Planned Introduction Date								
Hold Phase Review Meeting								

Functional Description		Responsibility	
PM	Project Manager	R	Responsible
M	Marketing	KP	Key Participant
R&D	Research & Development (Design Engineer)	A	Attend or Participate
O	Operations (Doc Control Purchasing, Materials, Proclamation, and so on)		
ME	Manufacturing Engineers		
E	Executive Sponsor		
CS	Customer Support		
Other	Legal, Finance, Quality		

KEY TO EXERCISE 3:
The Design Phase—Roles and Responsibilities

Note: The suggested answers represent a summary of several different companies and may vary from company to company. The task list is by no means comprehensive, and should be customized to fit your company's environment.

Tasks	PM	M	R&D	O	ME	E	CS	Other
Hold Design Reviews for								
Assemblies	KP	KP	R	KP	KP			A
Sub-Assemblies	KP	KP	R	KP	KP			A
Purchased Parts	KP	KP	R	KP	KP			A
Software	KP	KP	R	KP	KP			A
Other								
Track Progression on all Key Plans (MFG, QA, ME, etc.)	KP	R	KP	R	R			R
Sign Alpha and Beta Site Agreement	KP	R	R		R			A
Release Product Drawings	KP		R	KP				
Release Assemblies and Sub-Assemblies	KP		R	KP	KP			
Release Software	KP		R					
Complete Alpha Test	KP	KP	R	KP	KP			A
Update Engineering Bill of Materials			R	KP				
Create Planning Bill of Materials	KP	KP	KP	R	KP			
Finalize Training Plans	KP	R	KP	R	KP			A
Update Approved Vendor List (AVL)	KP		KP	R				
Update Pro Forma P&L	R	KP	KP	KP				KP
Confirm Planned Introduction Date	KP	R	KP	KP	KP			
Hold Phase Review Meeting	R	KP	KP	KP	KP	KP	KP	KP

Functional Description		Responsibility	
PM	Project Manager	R	Responsible
M	Marketing	KP	Key Participant
R&D	Research & Development (Design Engineer)	A	Attend or Participate
O	Operations (Doc Control Purchasing, Materials, Proclamation, and so on)		
ME	Manufacturing Engineers		
E	Executive Sponsor		
CS	Customer Support		
Other	Legal, Finance, Quality		

70

EXERCISE 4:
The Manufacturability Phase—Roles and Responsibilities

Instructions: Indicate in the table below who is responsible for each task and who are the key participants and attendees. In the blank lines at the bottom you can list tasks that are specific to your company or project.

Tasks	PM	M	R&D	O	ME	E	CS	Other
Manuals Complete								
Service								
Operations								
Customer								
Beta Testing Complete								
Work Centers Ready								
BOM Loaded								
Order Entry, MPS, MRD Ready								
Operation Training Complete								
Planned Announcement Date								
Hold Phase Review Meeting								

Functional Description		Responsibility	
PM	Project Manager	R	Responsible
M	Marketing	KP	Key Participant
R&D	Research & Development (Design Engineer)	A	Attend or Participate
O	Operations (Doc Control Purchasing, Materials, Proclamation, and so on)		
ME	Manufacturing Engineers		
E	Executive Sponsor		
CS	Customer Support		
Other	Legal, Finance, Quality		

KEY TO EXERCISE 4:
The Manufacturability Phase—Roles and Responsibilities

Note: The suggested answers represent a summary of several different companies and may vary from company to company. The task list is by no means comprehensive, and should be customized to fit your company's environment.

Tasks	PM	M	R&D	O	ME	E	CS	Other
Manuals Complete								
Service	KP	KP					R	
Operations	KP	KP		R				
Customer	KP	KP		KP			R	
Beta Testing Complete			R					
Work Centers Ready	KP			KP	R			
BOM Loaded	KP			R				
Order Entry, MPS, MRD Ready	KP			R				
Operation Training Complete	KP			R				
Planned Announcement Date	KP	R					KP	
Hold Phase Review Meeting	R	KP	KP	KP	A	KP	A	

Functional Description		Responsibility	
PM	Project Manager	R	Responsible
M	Marketing	KP	Key Participant
R&D	Research & Development (Design Engineer)	A	Attend or Participate
O	Operations (Doc Control Purchasing, Materials, Proclamation, and so on)		
ME	Manufacturing Engineers		
E	Executive Sponsor		
CS	Customer Support		
Other	Legal, Finance, Quality		

EXERCISE 5:
The Introduction Phase—Roles and Responsibilities

Instructions: Indicate in the table below who is responsible for each task and who are the key participants and attendees. In the blank lines at the bottom you can list tasks that are specific to your company or project.

Tasks	PM	M	R&D	O	ME	E	CS	Other
Order Entry Ready								
Field Training Complete								
Product Announcement Made								
Sales/Marketing Literature Complete								
Service Manuals Distributed								
Production Ready								
Pro Forma P&L Updated								
Postmortem Review Started								
Product Transition Review								
Hold Phase Review Meeting								

Functional Description		Responsibility	
PM	Project Manager	R	Responsible
M	Marketing	KP	Key Participant
R&D	Research & Development (Design Engineer)	A	Attend or Participate
O	Operations (Doc Control Purchasing, Materials, Proclamation, and so on)		
ME	Manufacturing Engineers		
E	Executive Sponsor		
CS	Customer Support		
Other	Legal, Finance, Quality		

KEY TO EXERCISE 5:
The Introduction Phase—Roles and Responsibilities

Note: The suggested answers represent a summary of several different companies and may vary from company to company. The task list is by no means comprehensive, and should be customized to fit your company's environment.

Tasks	PM	M	R&D	O	ME	E	CS	Other
Order Entry Ready	KP			R				A
Field Training Complete	KP							
Product Announcement Made	KP	R					KP	
Sales/Marketing Literature Complete	KP	R					KP	
Service Manuals Distributed	KP	KP					R	
Production Ready	KP			R				A
Pro Forma P&L Updated	R	KP	KP	KP				A
Postmortem Review Started	R	KP		KP		KP		
Product Transition Review	KP	R	KP	KP	KP	KP	KP	A
Hold Phase Review Meeting	R	KP	KP	KP	KP	KP	KP	

Functional Description		Responsibility	
PM	Project Manager	R	Responsible
M	Marketing	KP	Key Participant
R&D	Research & Development (Design Engineer)	A	Attend or Participate
O	Operations (Doc Control Purchasing, Materials, Proclamation, and so on)		
ME	Manufacturing Engineers		
E	Executive Sponsor		
CS	Customer Support		
Other	Legal, Finance, Quality		

74

EXERCISE 6:
The Postmortem Phase—Roles and Responsibilities

Instructions: Indicate in the table below who is responsible for each task and who are the key participants and attendees. In the blank lines at the bottom you can list tasks that are specific to your company or project.

Tasks	PM	M	R&D	O	ME	E	CS	Other
Product Transition Phase Complete								
P&L Review of First Months Result								
Review of Issues that Impacted NPI								
Product Cost Review								
Product Schedule Review								
ECO Review								
Review of Customer Feedback								
Manuals								
Internal								
External								
Review of Product Quality								
Review of Customer Feedback								
Product Quality								
FABs								
Review and Update of Customer Survey Questions								
Formally Schedule Postmortem Meetings over the Next Three to Twelve Months								

Functional Description		Responsibility	
PM	Project Manager	R	Responsible
M	Marketing	KP	Key Participant
R&D	Research & Development (Design Engineer)	A	Attend or Participate
O	Operations (Doc Control Purchasing, Materials, Proclamation, and so on)		
ME	Manufacturing Engineers		
E	Executive Sponsor		
CS	Customer Support		
Other	Legal, Finance, Quality		

KEY TO EXERCISE 6:
The Postmortem Phase—Roles and Responsibilities

Note: The suggested answers represent a summary of several different companies and may vary from company to company. The task list is by no means comprehensive, and should be customized to fit your company's environment.

Tasks	PM	M	R&D	O	ME	E	CS	Other
Product Transition Phase Complete	R	KP	KP	KP	A	KP	A	R
P&L Review of First Months Result	R	KP	KP	KP	A	KP	A	KP
Review of Issues that Impacted NPI	R	KP	KP	KP	A	KP	A	
Product Cost Review	R	KP	KP	KP	A	KP	A	
Product Schedule Review	R	KP	KP	KP	A	KP	A	
ECO Review	R	KP	KP	KP	A	KP	A	
Review of Customer Feedback	R	KP	KP	KP	A	KP	A	
Manuals								
Internal	KP	KP	KP	R	A	KP	A	
External	KP	KP	KP	KP	A	KP	KP	
Review of Product Quality	KP	KP	KP	KP	A	KP	A	R
Review of Customer Feedback	KP	R	KP	KP	A	KP	A	
Product Quality	KP	KP	KP	KP	A	KP	A	R
FABs	KP	R	KP	KP	A	KP	A	
Review and Update of Customer Survey Questions	KP	R	KP	KP	A	KP	A	
Formally Schedule Postmortem Meetings over the Next Three to Twelve Months	R	KP	KP	KP	A	KP	A	

Functional Description		Responsibility	
PM	Project Manager	R	Responsible
M	Marketing	KP	Key Participant
R&D	Research & Development (Design Engineer)	A	Attend or Participate
O	Operations (Doc Control Purchasing, Materials, Proclamation, and so on)		
ME	Manufacturing Engineers		
E	Executive Sponsor		
CS	Customer Support		
Other	Legal, Finance, Quality		

QUESTIONS . . .

1. List the six phases of the NPI process, as outlined in this book.

   _____

   _____

   _____

   _____

   _____

   _____

2. List the major objectives of the concept phase.

   _____

   _____

   _____

   _____

   _____

3. List five tasks that are performed during the concept phase.

   _____

   _____

   _____

   _____

   _____

4. List five tasks that are performed during the investigation phase.

   _____

   _____

   _____

   _____

   _____

5. What are the two major objectives of the design phase?

_____

_____

_____

_____

_____

6. List three tasks that are performed during the design phase.

_____

_____

_____

_____

_____

7. What are the major objectives of the manufacturability phase?

_____

_____

_____

_____

_____

8. List five major tasks that are performed during the manufacturability phase.

_____

_____

_____

_____

_____

QUESTIONS . . . (continued)

9. List the purpose of the postmortem phase.

_____

_____

_____

_____

_____

10. List three topics that should be included in the postmortem review.

_____

_____

_____

_____

_____

...AND ANSWERS

1. The concept phase
    The investigation phase
    The design phase
    The manufacturability phase
    The introduction phase
    The product transition and postmortem phase

2. Explore the technical and market potential to meet customer
    expectations
    Decide if the product development will go forward
    Develop a competitive analysis

3. Write the market requirements document (MRD)
    Write the engineering requirements specifications (ERS)
    Develop a project plan with a time table
    Hold a phase review meeting
    Hold program kick-off meeting

4. Establish the parameters of the new product project
    Conduct a customer survey
    Write the product transition plan
    Update the initial project plan with a detailed task list and times
    Develop quality plans

5. To prove the integrity of the design
    To test the manufacturing processes by producing units in a
    production environment

6. Alpha and beta site selection and testing
    Marketing loads the forecast
    Develop and update the engineering bill of materials (BOMs)

7. To determine the capability to plan, buy, build, test, install, and service
    the product, based on the engineering BOM
    To evaluate new product performance (including technical performance,
    reliability, and service) and customer satisfaction at the customer site

... AND ANSWERS (continued)

8. Work centers are ready—routing is compiled

BOM is loaded

Operation training is completed

Order entry, MPS, and MRP are ready

Phase review meeting is completed

9. Evaluate how well the new product works

Evaluate how well the product processes worked (Manufacturing, Order Entry, and so on)

Document the learning that took place

10. Review and update the customer survey

Review all ECOs, their cost, and cause

Compare cost projections with actual and document suggested improvements

Review major issues/problems that impacted the project, establish root causes, and take corrective action

M O D U L E

V

Conclusion—
Breakthrough Thinking

EMBRACING CHANGE

Change and the individual's willingness to create change are among the major prerequisites for an organization's continuous success.

Critical ingredients that drive the change process include:

- A commitment to continuous process improvement, along with continuous learning

- A shared sense of purpose as outlined in the business plan

- An organization's ability to stay focused, while maintaining an attitude of flexibility

- Open communication

Continuous process improvement requires a mindset in people that is typified by looking for ways to make things better. It requires people who are willing to break out of preconceived ways of doing things, the standards, and embrace the idea that levels of excellence keep getting higher.

Another critical item in creating change is the establishment of an environment of continuous learning. People must be selected who want to learn and are willing to share information and work as members of a cross-functional team. There must also be a reward system in place that recognizes people for their problem-solving skills, innovative ideas, team work, "peer" customer satisfaction, and so on.

In order to create this type of environment, the management team must assume the roles of coach and trainer. Jobs must be structured so that learning takes place instantly. Tools such as computers, software, and training must be part of the change environment.

People must understand the reason the company is in business. This purpose must be communicated through the business plan. People must understand the challenges as well as the competitive pressures the company is faced with. The executive team likewise must understand the challenges and pressures its people are faced with. One without the other may be a competitive disadvantage when trying to select the best people in the future. People must understand how they fit in, how they will share in the gains, and why change is good for them and the company.

EMBRACING CHANGE (continued)

People and organizations must become more and more responsive to marketing and customers. They must be able to do risk assessments, then minimize decisions that lock the organization in. They must be able to identify alternatives, and make decisions without cutting off other options.

The most important thing is a willingness to evaluate the way things are currently being done, and search for better ways.

Finally, for change to be accepted, there must be communication. Those individuals that are directly affected must be consulted. Those that are least affected should be informed.

Remember, objections thrive on resistance; they die on acceptance.

CREATING CHANGE

In order to create an environment for change, consider the following. Change must be driven from the top down. There must be a designated leader whose major responsibility is to champion the changes required and identify the adequate resources in terms of people, funding, systems, equipment, and so on.

The education and training strategy and related curriculum and delivery mechanics must be put in place to provide the reinforcement needed to accomplish change and reinforce the behavioral change desired.

In order to create change, an adequate system of support must be established. The first step is to identify the stakeholders. These are the individuals who must be convinced that a certain change is necessary. These stakeholders are made up of the managerial team, customers, and suppliers. The second major step is to involve employees in the change process through communication and participation.

BREAKTHROUGH THINKING

Breakthrough thinking serves as the catalyst for creative, "out-of-box" thinking that stimulates new ideas for products, services, processes, and so on.

In order to achieve breakthrough thinking, teams and organizations need to have individuals with breakthrough thinking skills, and a process in place that documents the various stages in breakthrough thinking and pushes for waste reduction.

The environment for breakthrough thinking could be categorized in the following ways: culture, vision in the business plan, leadership and management structures, individual skill sets, and supporting technologies.

The executive team faces two potentially contradictory challenges in creating an environment that enables breakthrough thinking: 1) changing things, and 2) trying to keep things from changing.

To support this, a system of process management must be put in place to standardize the process. Standardizing the process keeps things from changing. Once the results can be predicted, a new environment is created that encourages change, and hopefully results in breakthroughs.

The control part of the equation creates a system that prevents change (parts that can be put together in only one way). It establishes a system that adheres to standards, targets, or norms, and reacts in the form of corrective action/ root cause analysis, when there are departures from the norm.

The breakthrough part of the equation, on the other hand, challenges these targets or norms by changing the process. Consider Figure 5-1.

When one looks at this chart, there are at least two questions to be asked: How do breakthroughs take place? How do you create breakthrough thinking faster and faster? The answer lies potentially in the creation of an environment for breakthrough thinking and the supply of the appropriate technologies to support this breakthrough thinking. In the latter case, establishing information systems (the Internet) has already been completed. There are numerous examples of companies already doing this.

Assuming the information technology is either in place or evolving, the next question deals with the actual establishment of the breakthroughs themselves. First, we must create the culture, then the management structure. Then, develop the people skills and continue to support the first three with the technologies.

Breakthrough Thinking

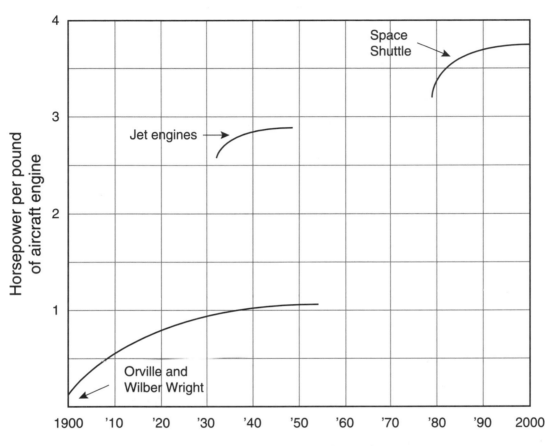

FIGURE 5-1. *Breakthrough thinking.*

BREAKTHROUGH THINKING (continued)

Following are seven simple steps that describe how the breakthrough process might take place.

| STEP 1 | Adopt a breakthrough attitude:

- Challenge the standards

- Make breakthrough thinking part of the business plan and functional strategies

- Establish a channel (process) for the flow of ideas (use both internal and external information networks)

- Establish a system of assigning people to new situations

- Make sure your reward system is reviewed and supports the entire organization

- Value people as key resources

- Develop abilities to embrace change

- Set an example for everyone else

- Create an organization for managing in an environment of equals

- Make participation in breakthrough thinking part of every job description

| STEP 2 | Identify products/projects. This is done during the business planning stage.

| STEP 3 | Organize for breakthroughs. This is accomplished by developing a team-based module that provides "time for individuals to think."

| STEP 4 | Create an environment of continuous learning, teaching people how to learn, and how to learn faster. Learning is a process. Document the process, then take the waste out of the learning and thought processes. Teaching people how to learn is a breakthrough in and of itself, which moves us closer to the "learning organization." |

| STEP 5 | Change the culture. This can also be looked at as a process. |

| STEP 6 | Document the change process and make it part of the business planning process. |

| STEP 7 | Control at one level and create breakthrough at the next level. When individuals and organizations reach this level, they are on their way to achieving continuous teaching. |

NOTES

NOTES

NOTES

NOTES

NOTES

NOW AVAILABLE FROM CRISP PUBLICATIONS

Books•Videos•CD-ROMs•Computer-Based Training Products

Subject Areas Include:

Management

Human Resources

Communication Skills

Personal Development

Marketing/Sales

Organizational Development

Customer Service/Quality

Computer Skills

Small Business and Entrepreneurship

Adult Literacy and Learning

Life Planning and Retirement

CRISP WORLDWIDE DISTRIBUTION

English language books are distributed worldwide. Major international distributors include:

ASIA/PACIFIC

Australia/New Zealand: In Learning, PO Box 1051, Springwood QLD, Brisbane, Australia 4127   Tel: 61-7-3-841-2286, Facsimile: 61-7-3-841-1580
ATTN: Messrs. Gordon

Philippines: Management Review Publishing, Inc., 301 Tito Jovey Center, Buencamino Str., Alabang, Muntinlupa, Metro Manila, Philippines   Tel: 632-842-3092,
E-mail: robert@easy.net.ph
ATTN: Mr. Trevor Roberts

Japan: Phoenix Associates Co., LTD., Mizuho Bldng, 3-F, 2-12-2, Kami Osaki, Shinagawa-Ku, Tokyo 141   Tel: 81-33-443-7231, Facsimile: 81-33-443-7640
ATTN: Mr. Peter Owans

CANADA

Reid Publishing, Ltd., Box 69559, 60 Briarwood Avenue, Port Credit, Ontario, Canada L5G 3N6   Tel: (905) 842-4428, Facsimile: (905) 842-9327
ATTN: Mr. Steve Connolly/Mr. Jerry McNabb

Trade Book Stores: Raincoast Books, 8680 Cambie Street, Vancouver, B.C., V6P 6M9
Tel: (604) 323-7100, Facsimile: (604) 323-2600
ATTN: Order Desk

EUROPEAN UNION

England: Flex Training, Ltd., 9-15 Hitchin Street, Baldock, Hertfordshire, SG7 6A, England   Tel: 44-1-46-289-6000, Facsimile: 44-1-46-289-2417
ATTN: M. David Willetts

INDIA

Multi-Media HRD, Pvt., Ltd., National House, Tulloch Road, Appolo Bunder, Bombay, India 400-039   Tel: 91-22-204-2281, Facsimile: 91-22-283-6478
ATTN: Messrs. Aggarwal

SOUTH AMERICA

Mexico: Grupo Editorial Iberoamerica, Nebraska 199, Col. Napoles, 03810 Mexico, D.F.
Tel: 525-523-0994, Facsimile: 525-543-1173
ATTN: Señor Nicholas Grepe

SOUTH AFRICA

Alternative Books, PO Box 1345, Ferndale 2160, South Africa
Tel: 27-11-792-7730, Facsimile: 27-11-792-7787
ATTN: Mr. Vernon de Haas